ZACH CALLIES

Rooted in Christ

Contents

Rooted in Christ

T rees are incredible plants that do a lot of things for us. Trees clean the air, provide necessary moisture, and support the wildlife. They allow us to make paper, various medicines, and even provide jobs for people. They grow tall and strong, withstanding rain, storms, and more, while bearing fruit and helping sustain some of our most necessary resources. However, the great and mighty plants cannot stand alone. Their wide trunks, and strong branches are not sustaining in themselves. Their strengthen is dependent on something that we can't always see. Something that lies beneath. They are dependent on their roots.

Without their roots, trees would fall. It is inevitable that they would cease growing, and fail to produce what we need. In fact, trees cannot grow and sustain themselves without the roots. They cannot grow and they cannot build, nor can they bear fruit. What we see of the tree, is completely dependent on what we can't see, the roots.

There are also many different species of trees. There are some trees that require warmer climates. Similarly, there are some that need cooler climates. Even the soil that the tree is planted in can drastically affect the tree, as well as how much sun, water and nutrients the tree receives. Where it's planted, and how it's fostered is very important to maintaining and strengthening the roots, and also producing a healthy tree.

It's often said that the tallest trees have the deepest roots. However, that is a misconception. What we can say though, is that the "strongest" trees often have the deepest roots. The tree or plant that has deep roots will not often fall, as it is supported by its roots, but the weak rooted tree will fall every time. The tree needs strong roots to grow and be fruitful for long periods of time.

Likewise, as Christians, it is very important that we make sure that we have our roots in the right place and growing. If our roots aren't in the right place, we won't grow. Like the tree, if we are not planted and rooted in Christ, we will seemingly "die", and cease to build further. If we don't have our roots in the right place, in Christ, then we will stop building, growing, and becoming more like Him. Just as a tree that fails to be rooted in solid, fertile ground, and nurtured rightly, we also will no longer bear fruit, and produce good things for the kingdom of God.

Our roots need to be in Christ. In every area of our lives, every root needs to go back to Christ. Our identity, should be rooted in Christ. Our strength should come from Christ. Even our love, joy, and peace should all be traced back to Christ.

When we are healthy Christians, rooted in Christ, we are similar to trees, or any plant. We grow stronger, bear good fruit, and provide good things for the world. But, like the trees and plants of the world, our strength depends on the strength of the roots. If we have strong roots in Christ, good fruit and life will naturally flow. However, if we have weak roots in Christ, or no roots at all, we will fall away at the slightest push of the wind, and become another tree fallen in the forest of this world.

Being rooted in Christ is not just a suggestion, or a nice tactic for living a Christian life. It isn't something we do out of religion. Nor something that we do because the church tells us it's a good idea. But it is essential to our lives in this world.

The Bible features many stories of men and women that were rooted in Christ. Of course, the Old Testament greats were not "in Christ", but rather they lived their lives "in faith". Although they didn't have Christ living on the inside of them like we do, they lived their lives having faith in the God of Abraham. However, many of the Old Testament greats, and the vast majority of the Jewish people at the time, didn't have the resources that we have today. They lived in faith, but they didn't have all of the stories, or direct, instant access to all that we have today. Yet, they were in faith, and lived their lives rooted in God.

Today, we have the living word of God, the Holy Spirit, and more, in addition to the experiences and teachings of others. These alone are far more than the Jewish people had, and more than the greats had. But, these greats had something that not all of us have had, and something that greatly impacted their faith.

There is a "hall of faith" found in the book of Hebrews, that lists those that "by faith" did great things. This passage includes Abraham, Jacob, and Moses, and more and it gives accounts of the their acting in faith. Those listed lived their lives in faith and were truly rooted in faith, rather than in this world. Furthermore, you could say that they were not only rooted in faith, but also, preemptively rooted in Christ, aside from the spiritual aspects of this, which we will discuss later.

Their great faith was shown through their acts. But they

didn't have the Bible. They didn't have teachings, and they certainly didn't have bible school or churches. What they had, in addition to the law, was personal encounters with the living God.

Abraham was given a promise from God, and made a covenant with Him. Jacob wrestled with God and God broke his hip, renaming him Israel, and brought from him a large nation from the twelve tribes of Israel. And Moses met God at the burning bush, and God appointed him to lead the Israelite out of captivity by Egypt, bringing the great Exodus.

Not everyone in the "hall of faith" had crazy stories like these, but they all, through others or themselves, had personal encounters with God. Those encounters with God, are what gave them the faith to step out and walk in boldness and obedience. They were rooted in faith and in Christ, based upon encounters, and oftentimes, personal relationship with God.

Likewise, we should be rooted in Christ, not based upon what we know, or what we have done, but through relationship with Christ. Relationship with Christ often looks different from what we expect though, and entails a variety of things. But, through this relationship, is where we are able to bury our roots deep in Him, and experience a growth in fruit, and faith.

Being rooted in Christ, we will no longer be stuck in the old ways, but we'll be transformed into a new image. The days of wavering from side to side in our faith will be short, and we'll stand firm in the faith, just as the Old Testament greats did before us. The promises of God will begin to take shape in our lives, and there will be fruit that none will deny, nor will they tear away. This new walk comes from having a relationship with God, and being rooted and established in him.

"As you therefore have received Christ Jesus the Lord, so walk in Him, rooted and built up in Him and established in the faith, as you have been taught, abounding in it with thanksgiving" (Colossians 2:6-7 NKJV).

Christians should be rooted in Christ. This is not just so that we may be able to stand tall against the weathering storms, or against the mighty winds. But so that we might bear fruit for God's kingdom, and be a blessing to this world.

"Blessed is the man
  Who walks not in the counsel of the ungodly,
  Nor stands in the path of sinners,
  Nor sits in the seat of the scornful;
  But his delight is in the law of the Lord,
  And in His law he meditates day and night.
  He shall be like a tree
  Planted by the rivers of water,
  That brings forth its fruit in its season,
  Whose leaf also shall not wither;
  And whatever he does shall prosper" (Psalm 1:1-3 NKJV).

Seed and Fruit

God created this world in all of its entirety. He created the oceans and the sands, the moon and the stars, the grass and the flowers. He created the birds, the snakes and the fish in the sea. God even created the night and day. One of the most impressive things he made though, was fruit.

Fruit is something that can be both bitter, and sweet. It can be crunchy like apples, and mushy like bananas. There are many different types of fruit and they are all so different, yet they are the same in that they are all fruit.

The thing that separates fruit from one another however, is the thing that we can't see. That which lies beneath the ground, beneath the dirt in which it is planted, is the seed. This is the difference maker when it comes to what fruit is borne.

Seeds that are planted in the ground dictate what is sprung up and borne as fruit. Without the seed, a tree won't be planted. The tree will never be sprung forth from the ground. The same can be said for a fruit without a tree. Without the tree, fruit will never be borne. If there is never a tree, a fruit won't just pop up from the ground and fall down from the sky. Thus, without first having and planting a seed, a fruit will never be borne.

If one wanted an apple, and there was not a store that was near, they can't just hope and pray for an apple and have it appear.

That would be unrealistic in the eyes of us all, impossible even. They also couldn't do the same for a tree, or a grape, or any other plant. It would take a miracle from God for that to happen, and this typically isn't the type of thing that warrants a miracle from God.

If someone wanted an apple, and they couldn't get one from the store, they would need to do some planting. They would need to find an apple seed, plant it in the ground, and wait. After some time of waiting and watering, an apple tree would begin to sprout, and after some more watering and waiting, apples would begin to grow. Now that the apple tree is alive, sprouted, and bearing fruit, it will continuously produce apples until it either dies, or gets taken from the ground. This is a process that most of us are familiar with, I'm sure.

Genesis 8:22 tells us this:

"While the earth remains, seedtime and harvest, cold and heat, summer and winter, day and night, shall not cease" (Genesis 8:22 NKJV).

Until the end of the age, while this earth is here, seedtime and harvest is a process that will never fade, never stop, and never cease. This means that in every situation, the process of planting a seed, waiting some time, and receiving a harvest, will never stop happening. We are always planting seeds, always waiting, and always seeing a harvest of some kind. The Bible is clear, that this is God's preferred method of bringing upon a harvest, and bearing fruit.

Now most of us are not going to end up becoming farmers, or even gardeners, so we won't be too familiar with this whole planting process. What we will all do though, is plant seeds in our lives, and in the lives of others. The process of seedtime and harvest doesn't cease in these instances either. We will plant seeds in our lives and the lives of others, and there will certainly be a harvest.

"How do we plant seeds?" may be the next question you're asking and there are many ways that we could answer that question. We can plant seeds when it comes to our finances, with the tithe, investing, and all sorts of other ways. Our words can become seed when we give our friends a good compliment. I know that a compliment from a friend has bore good fruit in my life from time to time. We can say words about ourselves, that will eventually start to effect the way we even see our own selves. There are many more examples that we could come up with, but I'm sure you're starting to get the point.

The thing we must note when it comes to planting seeds though, is that the seeds will always produce a harvest, and the harvest will always be "like its own kind".

If we look at fruit once again, we will start to see that only apple trees can produce apples, and only apple tree seeds will produce apple trees. You won't see a lemon that's borne from an apple tree, nor an apple borne from a lemon tree. The seed has the potential to produce fruit that is in its likeness, and nothing more.

Let's look at a couple verses regarding this matter.

"Let this mind be in you which was also in Christ Jesus, who, being in the form of God, did not consider it robbery to be equal with God, but made Himself of no reputation, taking the form of a bond servant, and coming in the likeness of men" (Philippians 2:5-7 NKJV).

"He is the image of the invisible God, the firstborn over all creation" (Colossians 1:15 NKJV).

What we have here may seem like a contradiction, but it is in fact, completely true. Describing Jesus, the verses tell us that He is both born in the likeness of men, and the image of the invisible God. According to theses verses, He is born like man, but somehow, is also the living image of God.

As confusing as that is, there is an explanation for that. Jesus, in his human form, is the fruit that was born of the seed of the Holy Spirit. If He is from the Holy Spirit, his deity must be that of God, as the seed is from the Spirit of God. But his body is human, because the seed was born from the soil of man. Therefore, He is both man and God, because He is the fruit of both together.

Fruit is just like the seed of what was planted. It has the same nature. Looking once more to the apple seed, you can't have an apple seed that bears lemons. The only possible fruit for an apple seed, would be an apple. The fruit is always "like" that of the seed, just as the apple is always "like" the apple seed.

We can see this concept play out a variety of different ways. For instance, people that grew up with money and privileged tend to act a lot differently than those that grew up with a lack of both. People that work out and eat healthy, tend to act, look, and feel very different than those that don't workout and don't eat healthy. Here, the fruit is similar a byproduct of the seed that was previously planted.

But let's look a little deeper. Look at those with mental health problems, such as depression and anxiety. They tend to look and act differently than those that have never struggled with depression, nor anxiety. With the rates of diagnosed depression and anxiety skyrocketing in the last couple of decades however, it's almost hard to tell who struggles with it, and who doesn't though. It's quickly becoming a universal issue.

I used to struggle with depression and anxiety, and I can tell you that there was definitely something that caused it. There was a seed that I was planting continuously that led to the struggles that I had. For me, it was negative, often fearful thoughts that I was thinking on. Constantly, my mind was being fed with anxiety-inducing thoughts. So much so, that it had no choice to produce a harvest of fear, anxiety, and depression. Eventually, new thoughts were planted in my mind, and a new harvest started to grow. However, it took the old thoughts and lies being cut down, for new thoughts to be planted and produce a harvest.

For other people, there may be a traumatic moment that planted a major seed leading to mental health issues. Others may have a lifetime of trauma that has planted a seed, that's just kept growing. Of course, it doesn't have to be drastic. It could just be a simple lie that you're believing that's taken root. But the thing that is true in every circumstance is that there is always a seed involved, and fruit to be borne from that seed.

Something that is very important to this matter is that it is actually the seeds that we or others have planted that is causing us harm. This is great, however, because we can know exactly what seeds are being planted, by just looking at the fruit that has been borne in our life. From there, we can learn to uproot bad seeds in our life, and began to plant new ones.

For instance, we can look at a professional bodybuilder and immediately recognize that they are:

1. Eating a lot of food.

2. Working out a lot.
3. Getting adequate rest and sleep.

If we know this, than we can emulate that in our own life, and expect a similar outcome, or at least a "like" outcome.

Similarly, we can look at our lives and recognize that the good and bad things in our lives can all be traced back to good or bad seed that has been planted. I know now that if I am feeling sad, that I am often thinking on things that make me sad, or I'm feeding my mind on sad things such as sad music or movies.

Oftentimes, things like depression, joy, or other physical or emotional reactions are clear to see, and the seed isn't too difficult to identify. But something that is harder for us to look at and see, is whether or not we are rooted in Christ.

Being rooted in Christ means that we have planted ourselves in Christ and developed roots in him, just like seed. It means that He is in our hearts, and we are in Him. But it also means that there is fruit that is born of Him in our lives. We don't just act like the rest of the world, but we act as if we are "like" Him. To know if we are rooted in Him, we simply must look at the fruit that is born of our life. Fortunately, we have been given a list of fruits, both of the Spirit and of the flesh. This list has been given to us in the book of Galatians. Let's take a look at them.

"Now the works of the flesh are evident, which are: adultery, fornication, uncleanness, lewdness, idolatry, sorcery, hatred, contentions, jealousies, outbursts of wrath, selfish ambitions, dissensions, heresies, envy, murders, drunkenness, revelries, and the like; of which I tell you beforehand, just as I also told you in time past, that those who practice such things will not

inherit the kingdom of God.

But the fruit of the Spirit is love, joy, peace, long suffering, kindness, goodness, faithfulness, gentleness, self-control. Against such there is no law" (Galatians 5:19-23 NKJV).

This passage, which a lot of us are probably familiar with, gives us two lists. The first list is one of the fruits of the flesh. These are the things that are borne when one is "in the flesh". The next list is one of the fruits of the Spirit. These are borne when one begins to walk in and live "in the Spirit", and are rooted in Christ.

From these lists, I'm assuming you can spot some "fleshly" fruits that you hate to admit that you portray. But certainly, there are also some fruits of the Spirit that you are producing in your life, such as joy or patience. I'm sure we can all see these traits are shown among the people around us. Maybe among our family and friends, and even ourselves. But we shouldn't judge anyone or ourselves by these fruits, but instead, we must use them the right way.

While there are some that use this passage of scripture as a sort of "blueprint" to living a "good" Christian life, it shouldn't be used as such, at least from what I can see. Nor should it be used to judge or condemn others. That way tends to lead to strife, contention, and comparison. Although it could be easy to use this passage that way, that's not going to lead to any good.

Instead, it should be used to examine ourselves. When we plant a seed in the ground, we know what we are planting, and we know that with the proper care and maintenance, it's going to produce a specific harvest. But what if we didn't know the type of seed we planted? Imagine if you found a random seed, and you decided to plant it, not knowing what would come of it. You gave it the proper care and it grew. Eventually, it produced a harvest and a lemon started to sprout from the tree. Immediately, you would be sure that the seed that was planted, was actually the seed of a lemon tree. You knew what was planted, by the fruit that was borne.

Jesus actually talked about this very thing in the book of Luke.

""For a good tree does not bear bad fruit, nor does a bad tree bear good fruit. For every tree is known by its own fruit. For men do not gather figs from thorns, nor do they gather grapes from a bramble bush""(Luke 6:43-44 NKJV).

Here, Jesus explains that you can't get bad fruit from a good tree, and you can't get good fruit from a bad tree. He also says that a tree is known by its fruit, proving that you can actually tell what seed was planted, or what tree was planted, based on the fruit that was borne.

The fruits of the Spirit, and of the flesh, seemingly point directly to what Jesus has taught here as well. This leads us to a very powerful conclusion. We can actually know whether we are rooted in the Spirit, or in our flesh, based on the fruit that we can see borne in our lives.

For instance, we can often see clearly if someone struggles with fits of anger or drunkenness. Those fruits are clear in our lives and when we struggle with them, others know. They would also be a clear sign that someone, in at least some area of their life, is not rooted in Christ, but is instead rooted in their flesh. Other struggles such as jealousy and idolatry may fly under the radar, however, but they are often clear to those that know you best.

In another case, there are many that exude the fruits of the

Spirit in their life. They exhibit true kindness and gentleness to others. Others may be extremely loving, and some are very patient. While only yourself and the Lord may know if the fruits that you show are real and true or not, that's typically a sign that someone is rooted in Christ.

If you're truly rooted in Christ, there will always be good fruit borne that people will see, and there will also be fruit if you're not rooted in Him.

The first step towards being rooted in Christ then, is pretty obvious. We must take a look at ourselves, and ask the question, "am I bearing the right fruit?"

I would encourage you to not only ask yourself that question, but to ask someone close to you as well. Ask a family member, a spouse, a friend, a mentor, or anybody that knows you and sees you as you are.

Be real with yourself, and allow others to be real with you. What kind of fruit are you bearing?

A New Nature

We live in a constant battle. One that, for the most part, goes very unnoticed. However, it can affect our lives as Christians more than nearly anything. It's a battle that we can't see, which is a trend we've seen before. Even still, we can see the effects of it play out, and we can feel it on the inside of us. This battle is that of our spirit versus our flesh.

Throughout the entire Old Testament, you'll only see the words, flesh and spirit, a handful of times, especially in the ways that you'll hear it discussed here. Instead, you tend to see physical war, man versus man violent, graphic war. You hear of stories like Samson, where a man with long hair fights and kills his enemies with his God-given strength. Or stories like that of David and Goliath, where a giant is killed by stones.

There is the story of Moses and the Israelites making it out of Egypt, away from their captors. The story of their exodus from Egypt ends with the Egyptian soldiers getting killed when going up against the red sea. The story also includes plagues of locusts, flies, and frogs. All of these are very real aspects of one of the greatest moments in human history, and they all consist of violence between men, and a physical conflict.

There are many conflicts between men in the Old Testament,

but very few that mention the spirit. Most of the conflict we see takes shape between men, whether they are complete enemies, or brothers. Its tough to find conflict between men and the demonic forces at work in this world, within the Old Testament. But looking at the New Testament, we can see that Jesus changed that dynamic completely.

Look back to the book of Genesis. In chapter 1 of the book of Genesis, we see that the Lord created Adam and Eve, after his likeness. We then see that they are given dominion over the entire Earth and over every creature that lives. Adam and Eve were essentially made gods of the Earth, of course, under the sovereign God. They were given authority over all that they saw, and the Lord saw that this was good. But of course the story takes a darker turn, when they are deceived by the Devil, who came in the form of a serpent.

The fall of man from the Garden brought upon many major changes for the first humans. They first became aware of both good and evil, recognizing the sin they had committed, and hiding from God. They no longer had the safety and blessing of the Garden of Eden, which was surely more beautiful and great than anything we have laid eyes on. What I have found to be very crucial though, is that they no longer had authority and dominion over the earth, and over every creeping thing.

While it is not explicitly stated that man lost his dominion, we can see in Luke 4:6, that dominion was delivered to the enemy in some sort of fashion. That is why you often hear the devil called "the god of this world", because he, technically speaking, has some sort of dominion over this world, and some of what goes on in it.

The only conclusion we can come to concerning this matter, is that Adam, now knowing both good and evil after disobeying

God, enslaved himself to sin. This essentially gave the enemy dominion over us for quite some time.

This is not a concept that is foreign to us. If I were to commit a crime right now and get caught, then I would be forfeiting my freedom, and spending some time in prison if the crime called for it. But I wouldn't say that God took that dominion away from me anymore than I would say that the lawmakers who created the law took my freedom away from me. I forfeited my freedom by committing the crime.

Likewise, Adam forfeited his freedom, and consequently, all of our freedoms for a time, by sinning in the first place. So, throughout all of the Old Testament and up until the time of Jesus' crucifixion, man lived enslaved to sin with no present hope of being saved and set free.

This, I find, is the exact reason why we only see conflicts between men in the Old Testament, and why we never see a spiritual conflict take place. If everyone is trapped in slavery by sin, then how can we even began to have a conflict with our spiritual captors. You don't often find prisoners successfully fighting and beating prison guards. How then can someone that is trapped in their sinful nature fight a battle against the sinful nature, or the spiritual oppressors? It simply can't happen. However, Jesus changed that.

Jesus, as we surely all know, died on the cross for our sins. In his perfect nature, he died for us, while we were still sinners. He was risen after the third day and defeated hell and the grave. Without him, we would still be enslaved to sin, like those that came before us. But, through the life and death, and life again, of Jesus, we were given many amazing blessings. We have eternal life, which is relationship with God. We have salvation, a way to Heaven. And we have a new spirit, one that is identical to that of Christ's. The new spirit that we were given, has a new nature.

For thousands of years, people were enslaved to sin, and had no choice but to conform to their sin nature, that is the flesh. The one thing that gave them any reason or way to fight it was the law. But the law didn't perfect them, and it didn't change their sin nature. The only thing it did was show their need for a savior, and give them a blueprint for what a sinless life could look like. But because of Jesus, we have a new spiritual nature.

This new nature isn't like the old nature. The old nature, that which was before our salvation, was enslaved to sin. It had no choice but to sin. It was in its nature. To try and truly change would be impossible on its own. It would be as if a lion tried to be like a sheep. While it could "act" like a sheep, it would never be able to push aside its predatory tendencies, and it would never submit to a shepherd as a sheep would. By nature, it is a lion, just as a sheep is a sheep by nature, regardless of how they act.

When Christ comes into our lives, and we accept him into our hearts, we allow him to completely transform our nature. We allow the old spirit and the old nature to die and a new Christ-like nature to live.

"I have been crucified with Christ; it is no longer I who live, but Christ lives in me; and the life which I now live in the flesh I live by faith in the Son of God, who loved me and gave Himself for me" (Galatians 2:20 NKJV).

When one receives salvation, and becomes a born-again believer, their old spiritual nature is crucified with Christ. It's as if they were on the cross with Christ on the day of his crucifixion, and their old man died. But they immediately are sprung up in life with Christ. For if one were to die with Christ, they would also likewise live with him, through him (Romans 6:8).

In this new life and with our new nature, we experience freedom. We are no longer slaves to our sin, and to our sin nature. We are, if anything, slaves to a truly pure spiritual nature. However, with this freedom in spirit, comes a challenge in the flesh.

Our new nature is not prone to sin, but prone to righteousness. It's not enslaved to sin, but enslaved to righteousness. We can't do anything about it, it simply is righteous and will continue to be that way. But when we are born again, and that change happens, it's not always evident.

Being born again doesn't mean that we change in our minds. The thoughts that one struggled with before being born again will be persistent after one is born again. Oftentimes, many of the same habits and sins will be stay the same immediately after salvation too. There isn't a change in your body either. One that is overweight before being born again will still be overweight after. The change that takes place in the salvation process that gives us a new nature is in our spirit.

But we are a three part being, made up of spirit, soul, and body. This is supported throughout scripture. God said in Genesis, that man is made in his image (Genesis 1:27). While some could interpret that in another way, the way that many interpret it is that man is made in three parts, as God is made in three parts. Spirit (the Holy Spirit), soul (God, the Father), and body (Jesus, the son). 1 Thessalonians 5:23 also gives us proof that we are indeed three parts.

"Now may the God of peace Himself sanctify you completely;

and may your whole spirit, soul, and body be preserved blameless at the coming of our Lord Jesus Christ" (Thessalonians 5:23 NKJV).

This verse very clearly states that we have three parts to us. We have our spirit, our soul, and our body. It is from our spirit that we experience the change at salvation. We don't experience it through our soul or our flesh. We experience it solely through our spirit.

This raises a challenge for us though. A challenge that is shown and discussed many times throughout the new testament. It is the challenge and battle between our perfected selves, in our spirit, and our non-perfected selves, our soul and body. This is the battle between our spirit and our flesh.

Our flesh is still like the old man and the old nature. It has never been perfected, and it won't be perfected until the end of the age. Therefore, our spirit and our flesh are in a constant battle. Righteousness vs sin. Life vs death. Spirit vs flesh.

We can see this conflict discussed throughout much of the New Testament. We see it through the fruits of the spirit vs the fruits (or works) of the flesh (Galatians 5). Jesus introduces us to this in Matthew's Gospel with the line, "the spirit indeed is willing, but the flesh is weak" (Matthew 26:41). We also see the conflict between our spirit and our flesh discussed throughout all of Romans 8. It is indeed a conflict, and one that we must be aware of.

We also must notice that this wasn't discussed in the Old Testament. We serve the same God that resides in the Old Testament, but this is not discussed. That is due to the fact that we had no control over this conflict before Jesus. When we were enslaved to sin in our old nature, we were utterly defeated.

There could be no conflict, because we, in our spirits, were with no hope and stuck in our sin nature. But because we have a new spirit, that has changed.

Like we've said, there can be no real conflict between a prisoner and their captors. When a prisoner is locked away, without a way to attack or defend themselves, there is no way that they can fight against their captors and win. Likewise, in our old nature, we were in complete captivity to sin. But Christ freed us, and gave us a new nature. That new nature allows us to no longer bow down to our previous captor, but we can walk in the freedom that Christ modeled.

Which is why we come again to the conflict between our spirit and our flesh. This battle is one that we must learn to fight, and that we must learn to win, if we are to be rooted in Christ. Fortunately, knowing that there is a battle that is taking shape is the first step in fighting the flesh, and a step closer to rooting ourselves in Him.

Spirit and Flesh

Imagine you visit an orchard. There, you see a beautiful apple tree with the best tasting and most attractive apples you have ever seen. You think to yourself, "I must find out what was used to make these apples!" So, you find yourself looking everywhere for the gardener and after searching, you finally find the gardener. You ask him all about the tree. What type of soil was used? How much sun? How much water? Finally, you ask about the seed. What do you expect him to say?

You would never expect him to answer with orange seeds, lemon seeds, or watermelon seeds. After all, he didn't reap a harvest oranges, lemons, or watermelons. He harvested apples. So, the only logical and possible answer would need to be apple seeds. When one plants a seed, they can expect the seed to naturally produce the same harvest as that of which they planted. Thus, when you ask the gardener about the tree, you can expect the answer to be: "an apple seed".

It's clear from fruit that has been harvested, that there is something like the fruit that has been planted. That is because the fruit or the harvest always comes from the seed that has been planted. It is not of its own, different DNA, but it has the same DNA as what has already been planted. It has no choice but to bear the same fruit as it has the potential to in its seed.

However, while trees, plants, and flowers work this way, we work a little bit differently. Seeds, by nature, are very simple. They are not dual minded. They cannot be both of the apple variety and the orange variety at the same time. They cannot bear the DNA of a lemon, while also bearing that of a pear. That is not how it works. They are a one part being, having no soul and no spirit. Seeds have only one part, and that is their physical form. But as we discussed already, we are a three-part being, consisting of spirit, soul, and body. Which undoubtedly makes things a bit more complicated.

We have a spirit, that has been made completely brand new (2 Corinthians 5:17). In that spirit, dwells the mind of Christ, truth, and perfect light. As Jesus is, so are we in our spirit.

However, in our body and our flesh, there is a desire and inclination towards sin. Our flesh is our bodily self that is connected and confined to the patterns of this world. The body must deal with the temptations and struggles that this present world has presented to us. This is shown, once again, through the life of Jesus. Jesus is and was always perfect, but He had to come down to our level to save us. He lowered Himself to the form of a servant, putting Himself under the limitations of a mortal body. Matthew 4:1 even tells us that Jesus was tempted.

"Then Jesus was led up by the Spirit into the wilderness to be tempted by the devil" (Matthew 4:1 NKJV).

This means that as Jesus walked this Earth, He dealt with the same temptations that you and I struggle with. Of course, he didn't have television or video games that he had to avoid, but He had the same temptations, just in a different way. But Jesus remained sinless, and as we certainly all know, we are not.

Galatians gives us an idea as to why.

"For the flesh lusts against the Spirit, and the Spirit against the flesh; and these are contrary to one another, so that you do not do the things that you wish" *(Galatians 5:17 NKJV).*

As we've said, the desires and the wants of the flesh are far different than the nature of the spirit. In the spirit, we are perfectly righteous, spotless, without a single blemish, just as Jesus is and always was. But in our flesh is all corruption. Our flesh is full of blemishes, and is not righteous one bit. Naturally, these two separate parts would start to oppose one another.

We ought not to stop there, however. I want you to think about the nature of these two things. The fruits can reflect their differences. Some of the fruits of the spirit include love, joy, peace, and patience. The fruits of the flesh however, include fits of anger, jealousy, and enmity. The spirit clearly only produces good fruit, while the flesh only produces bad fruit. But also, the fruits of the flesh are all aggressive. They push against others and press, causing issues, fights, and division. The flesh even pushes against you and I. It tempts you, and it makes its voice heard. While the spirit, although it does speak through convictions, wants you to come to it. It invites you in, not pulling and not pushing. It doesn't force its own way, as the flesh often does.

The spirit and the flesh are both parts of who we are, but the flesh is the natural way of us living. We've lived by the flesh since we were born. The things of this world, such as greed, envy, and fits of anger were in us as children and only are fostered as we grow older. Idolatry and rivalries develop as we grow, and many adults struggle with those bad fruits throughout their entire lives. These fleshly desires have been pushed and pressed into us our entire lives. But the things of the spirit have not been.

How often do you find a child that loves to be patient? Or a teen that is naturally kind? Not many adults these days even experience real joy. Judging simply by what we can see, it's safe to say that the things of the spirit are completely contrary to the natural way that we do things. So, how did Jesus do it? How did he remain perfectly sinless, even during times of temptation?

I find it best to look towards the wilderness season of Jesus. In the fourth chapter of the book of Matthew, we find Jesus being led into the wilderness by the Holy Spirit. In the previous chapter, Jesus was baptized by John the Baptist, and the Holy Spirit descends upon Him like a dove. So, from this moment in Jesus' life, to His ascension into Heaven, the Holy Spirit is upon Him. The full power of the living God rests upon Him. That's important to remember, because the Holy Spirit, as born again believers, is now a part of us too.

"Then Jesus was led up by the Spirit into the wilderness to be tempted by the devil. And when He had fasted forty days and forty nights, afterward He was hungry" (Matthew 4:1-2 NKJV).

After this powerful moment, The Holy Spirit leads Jesus into the wilderness. He walks through the wilderness for forty days with nothing to eat, and as you can surely imagine, He grows hungry. This is where the devil starts to tempt Jesus. He tempts Jesus three different times. The first was with bread.

"Now when the tempter came to Him, he said, "If You are the Son of God, command that these stones become bread."

But He answered and said, 'It is written, 'Man shall not live by bread alone, but by every word that proceeds from the mouth of God'''' (Matthew 4:3-4 NKJV).

The second temptation involved pride.

"Then the devil took Him up into the holy city, set Him on the pinnacle of the temple, and said to Him, 'If You are the Son of God, throw Yourself down. For it is written:
'He shall give His angels charge over you,'
and,
'In their hands they shall bear you up,
Lest you dash your foot against a stone.' "
Jesus said to him, 'It is written again, 'You shall not tempt the Lord your God' ''' (Matthew 4:5-7 NKJV).

And the last thing that the devil tempted Jesus with was glory and authority.

"And he said to Him, "All these things I will give You if You will fall down and worship me."
Then Jesus said to him, "Away with you, Satan! For it is written, 'You shall worship the Lord your God, and Him only you shall serve'''' (Matthew 4:9-10 NKJV).

After Jesus rejected every temptation, the devil departed from Him, and Jesus was ministered to by the angels before beginning His ministry.

The story of Jesus' temptations has been used to teach many lessons. One thing that you could notice is that Jesus only used scripture as his defense. With each temptation, Jesus used a verse from the Bible to aid him against the devil. He didn't try and use willpower or argue with the enemy. He only used the word of God to defend himself.

You could also point out that every temptation includes something that we tend to struggle with as Christians today. We all need to eat, and we all have urges. Jesus got hungry just as we do, and I'm not sure that I could go forty days without food as He did. We also tend to struggle with pride, and the desire for more authority and praise. Every temptation that Jesus was faced with, we also face today. Although that is a good point to make, and something we should learn from, there is something else that I would like to specifically focus on.

Throughout this entire situation, Jesus had a choice to make. He wasn't on autopilot like a robot. He was a real person who was faced with real temptations. Jesus wasn't on auto-perfect mode. Although it is difficult to imagine, He had a normal human body, and His body wasn't given special grace. Jesus had to struggle and He had to resist. He was faced with a very real choice, among difficult circumstances, which is not unlike what we experience today.

While I do not want to dismiss the divinity of Jesus, we must understand that in His mortal, not yet perfected body, He had the same needs that we have. There are some that would argue that the "temptations" weren't really tempting to Jesus, as He was still divine and perfect.But the Word of God is clear. Jesus went through temptations, just as we would. So, in His divinity, He still struggled with the bodily temptations that we deal with, yet, He overcame them.

"No temptation has overtaken you except such as is common to man; but God is faithful, who will not allow you to be tempted

beyond what you are able, but with the temptation will also make the way of escape, that you may be able to bear it" (1 Corinthians 10:13 NKJV).

God gave Jesus, as He also gives us, a way of escape when facing the temptations. Notice that Jesus didn't just run away from the devil, neither did He ignore him, though those would be the most obvious ways to escape the temptations. But He was able to say no and decide not to give in to his temptations. The theology of some is that we must always flee temptation. However, Jesus didn't model that here. He stood his ground and still escaped the temptations that He faced.

Think back to the baptism of Jesus. In Matthew, we see that the Holy Spirit descended upon Jesus like a dove to come and rest on him. From this point on, Jesus no longer walked in the power of man anymore, but He walked in the power of the Holy Spirit.

"When He had been baptized, Jesus came up immediately from the water; and behold, the heavens were opened to Him, and He saw the Spirit of God descending like a dove and alighting upon Him" (Matthew 3:16 NKJV).

This moment became a shift in the life of Jesus. With the power of the Holy Spirit, Jesus was now ready to begin His ministry and start doing signs, wonders, and miracles. But instead of immediately sharing the good news and making disciples, Jesus is led into the desert to be tempted. The reasoning behind this unimportant to the topic at hand, but the outcome is not. Jesus was able to withstand the temptations, but He did so after being given the power of the living God. With the Holy Spirit resting upon Him, Jesus was able to resist. This reflects that fact that the Spirit is necessary in the battle to resist temptation, both for Jesus, and for us.

In the temptations and trials that we face in life, we must have the Holy Spirit, and learn to walk in the Spirit, being rooted in Him, in order to be successful in resisting those challenges. We must *choose* to be in the Spirit, and choose not the things of the flesh. But in order to do that, we must make a decision, just as Jesus did in the wilderness.

"I say then: Walk in the Spirit, and you shall not fulfill the lust of the flesh" (Galatians 5:16 NKJV).

By choosing to walk in the Spirit, Jesus choose not to gratify the desires of the flesh. While He was in the wilderness, Jesus had to escape temptation, and while He could've ran away from the devil, or closed his ears and refused to listen, Jesus instead chose to walk in the Spirit, whom descended on him forty days prior at his baptism.

In our life, we must do the same. We must begin to resist our flesh, not by trying to run away from it, as that would be impossible. Neither by white-knuckling it, as we didn't see Jesus model that either. What we must do is walk in the Spirit, just as Jesus did, and choose the things of God, not the things of the flesh.

Now, I understand, that being told to walk in the Spirit, is not new to you, neither is it all that helpful. At least not without further explanation. So, we will spend time on that matter, later. But what we need to understand, is that being rooted in Christ, is the very beginning of walking in the Spirit. This all starts, however, with deciding the things of God, not the things of the flesh.

Mind and Choice

As we've already discussed, we are made up of three parts. We have a spiritual nature, a soul, and a body (1 Thessalonians 5:23). Our spiritual nature is hard to understand, as it is something that we cannot see and science cannot currently put a finger on. But as Christians, we have some insight on some very important aspects of the spiritual nature.

We know that it is no longer enslaved to sin, but that it is alive and connected to God (Romans 6:10). We also have the understanding that our spiritual self, bears the mind of Christ, and that it has the capability and nature to produce the fruits of the spirit, which are undeniably good things. So, we can also say that our spirit is identical to that of Christ, because it is both good in nature, and has the mind of Christ. Scripture also goes along to prove that in multiple other instances.

Our body, which we can also refer to as the flesh, bears a different nature however. One that is contrary to our spirit (Galatians 5:17). Unfortunately, the flesh is something we are all too familiar with, as it is the source of many of our desires, lusts, and cravings. For example, our body craves food. Without food, it would fail to survive. But someone that struggles with overeating would have a stronger desire and craving for food, which is why they tend to overeat. This desire and craving comes from our flesh, not our spirit. That is not all, however. The flesh is also our connection to this world.

As our spiritual nature longs to show us, we are more than just flesh and blood, although flesh and blood is all that we can visually see. We are spiritual beings as well as physical beings.

You have probably heard it said that we are really just spiritual beings, inside of a human body. While that's not completely correct, I agree with that to an extent. We do have a spiritual nature, but our body has been created by God for a purpose. It is important, and does play a crucial role in our walk on this earth. The body cannot be denied or ignored altogether, and neither can its purpose. Unfortunately though, it was corrupted long ago.

When Adam and Eve fell from grace, they had the same three parts, just as us. Spirit, soul, and body. But their spirit had been corrupted and been made a slave to sin, which then affected the rest of humanity. As their spirit became enslaved to sin, thus their body became of vessel of unrighteousness, a tool for the enemy and sin. But, when Jesus came and gave Himself up for us, He gave us access to a new-creation spirit and freedom from sin. So, our bodies were no longer made tools for unrighteousness, just as our spirits were no longer enslaved to sin.

"And do not present your members as instruments of un-righteousness to sin, but present yourselves to God as being alive from the dead, and your members as instruments of righteousness to God" (Romans 6:13 NKJV).

Our bodies are no longer enslaved and made undeniable tools for unrighteousness. Because our spirit was freed, there is a way for our body is escape slavery as well, and be made a tool for righteous. This means that there is a way for the body to act as a tool for Christ, although it has previously been a tool for the world.

However, the flesh is still weak and is not made perfect as the spirit has been made perfect. When I gave my life to Christ, my spirit was made new and made identical to that of the spirit of Jesus, but I didn't lose all of my belly fat and become the healthiest person that had ever lived. Thus, my body still has urges and desires that are contrary to that of my spirit.

Now, this is where our soul comes into play. Our soul is made up of our mind, will, and emotions. It is the part of reality outside of our body, that we are actually familiar with. When you think, it is with your soul. When you make a decision, it is with your soul. When you feel an emotion, it is with your soul. The single most important decision that you will ever make is to give your life to Jesus and accept that He is your lord and savior. This decision is not made with your spirit, although scripture does say that your spirit bears witness with the Holy Spirit. It is clearly not made with your body. But it is made with your soul. Right now, as you are reading this, you are reading and thinking about these words with your soul, and more precisely, your mind. It is in your soul and your mind that decisions are made, and where the war between your spirit and your flesh is truly fought.

The Bible speaks about your spirit, particularly in the New Testament, and it certainly speaks a lot on the flesh as well. Even the conflict between the two is brought up on multiple occasions, within the New Testament. But some of the most powerful and transformational verses are that which reference the mind. Like Romans 12:2 for example.

"And do not be conformed to this world, but be transformed by the renewing of your mind, that you may prove what is that good and acceptable and perfect will of God" (Romans 12:2 NKJV).

This verse refers to the renewal of one's mind. Through this verse, we can see that it is with the mind, and the renewal of such, that one is transformed and able to discern the will of God. The spirit certainly has some play in this, but the transformation that we go through as believers comes by the renewal of one's mind. Not through one's outward bodily acts, or a major spiritual experience, outside of the salvation one, of course.

The mind has the power to transform one's entire life, and it is by the renewal of one's mind that this takes place.

"For those who live according to the flesh set their minds on the things of the flesh, but those who live according to the Spirit, the things of the Spirit. For to be carnally minded is death, but to be spiritually minded is life and peace" (Romans 8:5-6 NKJV).

This passage tells us that setting your mind on the things of the Spirit is crucial to living according to the Spirit. Thinking on the things of the Spirit and controlling where your thoughts lean towards is the deciding factor as to if you will live according to the Spirit, or whether you will live according to the flesh. Whether you display the fruits of the Spirit - love, joy, patience, and more - is determined by if you set your minds on that of the Spirit. In other words, whether or not you are rooted in Christ is determined by your mind, and what you choose to think. If we want to be rooted in Him, living through Him, and displaying Him in the way we live our lives, we must take hold of our mind and present it to Christ with our thoughts.

Pastor and Author, Craig Groeschel, wrote in his book, *Winning the War in Your Mind*, that "the battle for your life is always won or lost in your mind." I believe that that holds true for everyone. The mind holds such a powerful place in our life, and it actually can decide what our outcomes in life will be. Just as the type of seed we plant determines the harvest that we will reap, the thoughts that we have inevitably determine the trajectory of our lives. Which is why we must acknowledge the battle that is taking place in ourselves, and in our minds particularly. The battle that wages between our spirit and our flesh.

This battle is easily seen. We often ask ourselves questions throughout our days. Some people ask themselves, "should I have that last slice of pizza?" Others may ask, "should I go into work today or just stay home?" These questions. and more, are certainly things I have asked myself from time to time. While they may be easily answered, they are still questions that we wrestle with. There is conflict and contention in our mind from these questions.

There are other questions however, that draw more con-tention, and more conflict in one's mind. There are many that ask the question, "is God real?" For some, it may be "do I deserve to be happy?" and for others, "should I even still be here?" These are questions that unfortunately plague the minds of many and have circulated my mind for a time. These are very real, tough questions, that must be answered. The truth with each and every one however, is that there is conflict, contention, and therefore a battle being waged. The answer to those questions is not decided in one's spirit however, nor is it in one's body, but in one's mind.

As we have discussed, we fight a war that is fought between our spirit, and our flesh. The spirit is willing, but the flesh is weak. The spirit has been made perfect, alive to God in Christ Jesus, while the flesh is corrupt and bound to carnal desires. The two are in constant opposition, but we have the chance to decide the outcome and the winner of this battle with the power of our mind.

It is in our minds that we decide if we will be rooted in Christ, and in the things of the Spirit, or if we will stay rooted in the flesh, as we did before we were redeemed by Jesus. With a simple choice in our minds, we can decide if our bodies will continue to be used for the kingdom of this world, or if they will be used for the glory of God. This is the decision that we will be consistently dealing with for the rest of our lives, and choice is something that we will consistently have to confront

Luckily, it is a decision that we are fully equipped to make, and the rest of our discussion will be focused on making that decision, by not only becoming better equipped, but by also renewing our mind to the Word of God.

"And do not be conformed to this world, but be transformed by the renewing of your mind, that you may prove what is that good and acceptable and perfect will of God" (Romans 12:2 NKJV).

Consider It So

I find it particularly important to next discuss the process that I would call "consider it so". This process is crucial in establishing your faith, and rooting yourself not only in Christ, but in the Word of God as well.

I recently spent much time in the Book of Romans. It is a very powerful book, that lays the foundations of grace and faith for Christians. Romans introduces us to ideas that the entire Old Testament leads to, and draws us back into deeper communion with God. It does this by instilling the idea that we are no longer enslaved to sin, and furthermore, no longer enslaved to the patterns of this world. We can live for God, because we have died to sin itself, and have been eternally connected to the Lord.

The passage of scripture that brought these ideas to life for me is in Romans 6.

"-knowing this, that our old man was crucified with Him, that the body of sin might be done away with, that we should no longer be slaves of sin. For he who has died has been freed from sin. Now if we died with Christ, we believe that we shall also live with Him, knowing that Christ, having been raised from the dead, dies no more. Death no longer has dominion over

Him. For the death that He died, He died to sin once for all; but the life that He lives, He lives to God. Likewise you also, reckon yourselves to be dead indeed to sin, but alive to God in Christ Jesus our Lord" (Romans 6:6-11 NKJV).

This passage begins with the idea that our old selves have been crucified with Christ, and are therefore, gone, done away with. We are no longer enslaved to sin like we were in the old self, but we have been set free for the point of living sin free. As Christians, we have the luxury of living for God, both internally, and externally with our actions.But the verse that makes everything click is verse 11, which states that we must "consider" ourselves dead to sin, and alive to God.

There is a truth on the inside of us, that if we are born again in Christ Jesus, then we are already dead to sin, and live to God. But it's common for us to see Christians enslaved to their sin even after having been born again. In fact, many of us would agree that most of the Christians in the world are failing to walk in the freedom and life that Christ offers through being born again. What is seemingly lacking then, is the process of considering yourself that way.

There is a truth on the inside of me that I am a man. Whether or not I would like to disagree, there is no changing that I am a biological male. But if I were to consider myself a different way, perhaps as one that is not a man at all, that would not change the fact that I am a man. The truth about me, is that I am a man, and that will never change. What changes from me considering myself differently then?

I would feel different, act different and live different. I would not be living in the truth, thus there would be an assortment of issues that I would inevitably face, due to the fact that I am choosing to live through the lies that I'm believing.

If a criminal were to consider it so that car theft is not against the law, they would face dire consequences, and end up in jail. What they consider to be the truth, isn't actually the truth, thus they are faced with issues and consequences. While these examples may seem extreme, we must understand that living and walking in the truth is very important, particularly for the Christian.

It would be easy for me to read the Bible and never consider that every word in that book is true. In fact, one could read the Bible and interpret it in a variety of different ones. You could read the Bible as a marvel of Jewish history, for example. It tells great stories, and gives great insight into the history that may otherwise go untold. There are some that read it as a book of wisdom, saying that they can follow Christian teachings, without following Christ himself. The Bible is truth is every one of the those circumstances. Whether you read it for the history, the values, or for the truth that it is, it's the truth regardless. But if you don't consider it the truth, then you will not be blessed or changed by it in the same way that you would be if you did consider it such.

The Bible is perfect, and it is the Word of God. When read in light of its truth, it has the ability to completely transform our lives and mindsets. It convicts us, teaches us, and trains us in the way that we should go. With it as our guide, we can truly walk in the life and freedom that Jesus has for us. But we must consider it the truth, and we must consider it the only truth.

A key part in the process of considering the Bible the truth is actually comparing it with the way that we think. For example, we may see ourselves as being unimportant or not cared for, but the Word says something different.

But you are a chosen generation, a royal priesthood, a holy nation, His own special people, that you may proclaim the praises of Him who called you out of darkness into His marvelous light" (1 Peter 2:9 NKJV).

Certainly if one is of a royal priesthood, they cannot be anything less than wanted. Here, the Word says something completely different about us, than what we say about ourselves. In order to get anywhere with ourselves, we must begin to consider what the Lord says as truth, not what we say or think, neither of ourselves, or of anything.

I once heard a story from a minister that would "rededicate" his life to the Lord at every single altar call. He had the understanding that he was a dirty sinner and needed to be forgiven every single week. He considered himself unsaved and in sin, thus that was the way he saw himself, and the way he believed God saw him. But in reality, God saw him as he saw every born again believer, that is, dead to sin, and alive to Him. Unfortunately, this is surely a belief that many believers have, and it springs from them not considering themselves as the truth itself considers them.

Scripture says that we have the mind of Christ. But if we don't consider the Holy Spirit as being of any use in your life, then the mind of Christ that we have won't be able to operate in our lives. We have a major blessing in the mind of Christ that dwells in our spirit man, but it won't ever act as a blessing if we never consider it so.

Another example that we could look at is healing. According to 1 Peter 2:24, we have already been healed and able to walk in that healing in our day-to-day life.

"who Himself bore our sins in His own body on the tree, that we, having died to sins, might live for righteousness—by whose stripes you were healed" (1 Peter 2:24 NKJV).

The verse does not say, "by his wounds, you can ask for healing and hope that you will receive it." It doesn't tell us to hope for a miracle, or to go to a healing conference and ask for it. It tells us that a miracle has already been done by Jesus with His sacrifice and resurrection. The miraculous work has already been done, and all that we have to do is consider ourselves healed, and our body will follow suit to our faith.

I have faith in Jesus Christ and consider him my Lord and my savior. If I didn't consider Him as such, then I would have no real faith in Jesus Christ. With no faith, I would never receive the salvation that the Lord offers. He gives of Himself, allowing us to be saved, but it takes receiving it by faith for us to be saved. It is the consideration or the belief that Jesus Christ is my Lord and Savior that deems me saved, not *just* the sacrifice that Jesus paid. Hence, to consider it so is of upmost importance if we are to be both rooted in Christ, and living by faith.

Considering something so doesn't just mean that are thinking of it a certain way. But in a broader sense, it means that we are taking into account what we can see, what we believe, and what we know as the truth. We are analyzing and determining what we will place our faith in, and what we will consider as truth. At times, these three things can all be the same, but at other times, they are all different.

For instance, I can see that the sky is blue, I believe it to be blue, and I know that as truth. But for the colorblind folk, the sky may not be blue, but pink or gray. They may know it to be blue based on the opinions and views of others, but they do not see it the same way that most of us see it.

There is a disorder known as body dysmorphia. It can cause people to see themselves differently than they really are. For example, those that have body dysmorphia may see themselves as being overweight, though they may be very underweight in reality. They could even step on the scale, see themselves as being underweight and still believe that they are overweight. In this case, what they see, is deterring them from what they know to be the truth. Thus, they are considering themselves overweight by what they see, not by the truth, which is that they aren't actually overweight

Let's apply this concept once more. Working out and exercise don't always produce an immediate result. In fact, we almost never see a physical change after just one workout. However, we know that working out changes our bodies and therefore we consider lifting weights and cardio to be changing our bodies, and helping us lose weight. We can see some results, such as weight loss, rather quickly, but the physical change happens over time, not instantly. If someone then wants to lose weight and get into shape, they would have to consider the daily workouts and nutrition needed to lose weight to be effective, regardless of what they see.

If we are to be rooted in Christ, however, we must take a look at what we can see and throw it out the window. Because as Christians, we don't live by what we see, but we live by faith.

"For we walk by faith, not by sight" (2 Corinthians 5:7 NKJV).

I've often used to wonder why God doesn't just appear or speak audibly to everyone. That would make it so easy to believe, and many more people would turn to God. We wouldn't need to go out and evangelize. We wouldn't need missionaries or anything like that. People would just believe and that would be okay. But it certainly wouldn't be.

Anybody can live by what they see. It's easy, and takes no effort on our part at all. But to have faith and believe is a challenge and it takes commitment. If God revealed himself physically to every single person, they would have no choice but to believe in God. It would be plain and clear for everyone to see that Jesus is real and worthy to be praised. But the choice that God gives us all allows us to foster real faith, and real commitment. Thus, for every Christian, we are not to live by what we can see, but by what we can't necessarily see, as that is the path that requires faith, and the path that requires God.

Now, we come back to consider it so, and there is a question that we must ask. What is the truth that we are to believe in? If we are not to place our consideration on the seen things of the world, then what are the unseen things to which we must place our faith?

I believe there to be an absolute truth, and I pray that you do as well. This truth can only be found in the Word of God, and in the words spoken through his Spirit.

"However, when He, the Spirit of truth, has come, He will guide you into all truth; for He will not speak on His own authority, but whatever He hears He will speak; and He will tell you things to come" (John 16:13 NKJV).

Jesus tells us that the Spirit of truth, whom we know resides inside of us, will come and will not speak on his authority, but on the authority of God, the Father. Therefore, the truth that we must cling to, that which we must consider, comes from two things, the Word of God, and the Holy Spirit.

Thus, this is where we must stay as we learn to become rooted in Christ. To truly root ourselves in Him, we must renew our mind, and this happens when we begin to consider His words, and consider them true. We must cling to them, hold onto them, and allow them to transform us.

"My son, keep your father's command,
And do not forsake the law of your mother.
Bind them continually upon your heart;
Tie them around your neck.
When you roam, they will lead you;
When you sleep, they will keep you;
And when you awake, they will speak with you" (Proverbs 6:20-22 NKJV).

Mediating on the Word

Being rooted in Christ, is the process of placing Jesus at the center of your life, and revolving your world around him. Rooting yourself in Him provides a harvest in your life that springs forth blessing, goodness, and life to not only yourself, but to all those around you. It changes us from the inside out and allows us to be transformed into the same image of Jesus, but not by striving and trying not to sin, but instead by focusing our attention on all of Him.

It requires us to place our identity no longer in the flesh, but in the Spirit. Not only that, it also requires us to take a look at the power of our mind and examine what we consider to be the truth. If we are believing something that is completely contrary to the truth, typically based on what we can see, then our eyes would no longer be on Jesus, but on the earthly things. Thus, we must look at the truth, and urge to place both our thoughts and beliefs on what we know to be true, rather than that which may *seem* to be true. This only happens if we know the truth.

As we've discussed, the truth can be found both in the Bible, and from the Spirit. Right now, most of us have immediate access to the scriptures. We can look them up on the Internet, take a look at the Bible app, or find a physical Bible to read. It's far more accessible than it's ever been, and at any point, we can turn to a page and find a verse. There are also countless books and resources from all around the world that can help with reading the Bible, and vast amounts of translations that make it easier to understand. There are ways to hear and listen to the Bible, and there are teachers that will teach it to you. With the wide range of options in the world, we simply have no excuse for not reading the scriptures.

But oftentimes, just reading the Bible is not enough for it to change you. If we look at the stories and the lessons in the Bible and we see them as we see any other book or resource, then it won't reap the harvest that we want. If we read it as fiction, it won't help us to change. If we read it like a study guide, it won't help our heart. Even if we were to read it like we would a self-help book, there wouldn't be much change that would take place spiritually. We have to read it within it's full context and power. We cannot limit the Bible to just being a book, or even a really good book at that. We must look at the Bible as the infallible Word of God, and we must consider it the absolute truth of our lives. Only when we view it as such, will we see the blessings that it reaps, and the change that it brings.

If you know the Bible as truth, and you know it as the Word of God, your next step is to get the truth to live on the inside of you. This comes, by mediating and spending time in the Bible itself. One of my favorite Proverbs reminds us of this.

"My son, keep your father's command,
  And do not forsake the law of your mother.
  Bind them continually upon your heart;
  Tie them around your neck.
  When you roam, they will lead you;
  When you sleep, they will keep you;

And when you awake, they will speak with you" (Proverbs 6:20-22 NKJV).

Think about your thoughts and what they tend to stay on. Are you mediating on the Bible, and keeping the Lord's words continually in your heart? Oftentimes, when we read our Bibles, we don't really meditate or think about what we are reading. Many of us may skim over it and try to digest what we can. Sometimes we can understand it, and sometimes we can't. But most of the time, we forget about it later when we start a new activity. We don't keep it on the forefront of our minds and mediate on it throughout our days as we should.

The Bible is something that needs to be thought about, and it needs to be meditated on. When we actually think through it, we allot our minds extra time to remember it, and we give ourselves a greater chance at letting the Bible dictate our thoughts. Knowing the power of your mind and the effect that our thoughts have on it, it should be clear that mediating and spending time invested in the Word will completely change our lives, simply by it changing our minds. By allowing ourselves to mediate on God's word, we dictate what we choose to think on, and we force our mind to adapt to the Word of God.

Also, the Word of God acts as a seed, and when we plant it into our thought-life and our minds, we begin to see a harvest of change on the inside of us. Thus, by mediating and spending time thinking on the Word, we begin to effortlessly change into the image of Christ. This is not done by trying not to sin, but by being molded and changed on the inside of our hearts, by the Word and truth itself.

Along with the Word of God though, we have a helper, the Holy Spirit. The Spirit lives on the inside of you and I, and is not only God himself, but also the Word of God.

"In the beginning was the Word, and the Word was with God, and the Word was God" (John 1:1 NKJV).

The Bible is not only true, but according to this verse, God himself. I understand it as being the written expression of God and His character, operating as his living Word, while the Holy Spirit is the Spirit of the living God. Luckily for us, because the Holy Spirit lives within us, as does the Bible, in a sense. This is helpful in understanding and knowing the scriptures as the Spirit operates in making what is already in our spirit come alive in our minds.

The Spirit also operates as a guide, leader, and teacher. As we can learn from the scriptures, so we can also learn from the Spirit. But additionally, the Spirit speaks to us, and often uses the scriptures to speak to us.

From the Spirit, we are convicted and shown areas that we need to work on, and areas where we are sinful. As we progress in our faith, we learn to listen more closely to the Spirit and its voice, which makes changing and sanctification much more seamless than before, when we first started to progress in our faith. The Spirit and scriptures work together on the inside of us to perfect us and morph us into the image of Christ. But, this can only be done when we meditate on the scriptures and allow them to live on the inside of our minds, and hearts. We have to know the Word for it to even be able to have an impact on our lives.

I've found that meditating on the Word is very practical. All it takes to start mediating is picking a scripture and spending time thinking about it. For instance, we could take a verse like

Romans 8:37, which says that we are "more than conquerors" through Christ, and meditate on it.

"Yet in all these things we are more than conquerors through Him who loved us" (Romans 8:37 NKJV).

When we are faced with trials, we can remember this verse and remind ourselves that we are more than a conqueror of the trial we are facing. Or, if we are feeling oppressed, we could pray, but we could also remember this verse and feel encouraged. Eventually, after reminding ourselves of this verse enough, we will just consider it the truth, and what were once trials, may be considered nothing more than a mere irritant.

We can do this with any scripture, although some may be more effective to meditate on than others. However, all scripture is "given by inspiration of God, and is profitable for doctrine, for reproof, for correction, for instruction in righteousness" (2 Timothy 3:16 NKJV). So, pretty much any scripture that you choose to meditate and think on will prove to be a blessing in your life, and bear a great harvest. The important thing is knowing the scripture that you need to mediate on.

Start by finding something that you are struggling with. It could be anxiety, depression, or family drama. Let's use money as an example. Imagine that you are in financial debt and nothing seems to being going well for you. Your job isn't great, and you don't get paid well to begin with. Maybe you're too busy to work a second job, or you have other major responsibilities. The natural way that we would look at this situation is to stress out, get into more debt, or just be totally complacent. But Philippians 4:19 tells us that God "shall supply all your need according to His riches in glory by Christ Jesus". Of course, you may not see where He is providing, but if you let your mind dwell on that verse, and you begin to consider it the truth, then eventually your faith will operate in your circumstances and God will provide for your situation. But in order for your faith to operate, and you to consider God as your provider, you must dwell on the truth and keep it in your mind. You can't consider what you neither know, nor remember, nor can you have faith for what you haven't already considered.

Just as your faith will not operate much without your considering and thinking on the truth, your mind will not be renewed either. Thus mediating on the Word of God, and placing it at the forefront of your mind will not only help your faith, and help you to know the truth, but it also plays a critical role in renewing your mind.

As we've already discussed, we are not transformed instantly by being born-again. Although that changes our spiritual nature, it doesn't change our body, nor does it change our mind. However, we are transformed by the renewal of our minds (Romans 12:2). This is a process, and it starts with mediating on and thinking about the truths that are found in the Bible.

We must learn and come to know the truth. This happens through the Word and through the Spirit, whom aids us in our understanding. By knowing and mediating on the Word, we will start to consider that which is found in scripture to be the truth, and so our faith will begin to operate.

It is through this process that we are transformed. Our lives will no longer look as they did before. We will no longer act, talk, or love like we did and there is new fruit that is ready to be born from our lives. Although we were once sinners, drunkards, and liars, we will now be joyful, patient, and kind. Of course, it is a process. But transforming your life and displaying new fruit starts with knowing and mediating on the truth.

However, there is one side of knowing the truth that we have not discussed. It is at the very heart of Christianity, and is crucial to fully understanding the truth, as well as displaying a sanctified, fruitful life that is rooted in Christ. In order to understand the truth and the Word of God, we must be in pursuit of knowing Him, and walking in relationship with Him. Only through knowing God, and abiding in Him can we begin to understand the Bible in it's fullness. It is relationship with God, truly knowing Him, that is at the center of placing your faith and foundation in Him.

Relationship With Christ

We've discussed what it means to be born again, and that your spirit has been made new to the Holy Spirit. We understand that we are no longer fighting a war with each other, but in fact, there is a spiritual war waging, as well as a war between our spirit and our flesh. This war with our flesh, makes it that we must make a choice in our mind, and that choice is whether we will be rooted in our fleshly nature, or our spiritual nature.

The process in making that choice starts with tackling what is in our mind. Our mind is filled with our thoughts, both conscious and subconscious, and what we choose to think and mediate on, will decide what we think about. If we do not choose to think on that of the truth, but instead, we think on the things of the flesh, then we will start to live out of our flesh, and remain rooted there. Thus, we must examine what we consider the truth, and what we choose to mediate and think on.

Thus, we have come to know that in order to be rooted in Christ, winning the spirit vs flesh battle and walking in the Spirit, we have to fully know the truth, and consider it to be so. This means that we have to read our Bibles and choose to think about the verses that we read, and choose to remember them.

Notice that everything comes down to choice. Whether or not we root ourselves in Christ, both in spirit and in our soul, is determined by us, and the choices that we continually make.

We also must come to know the one that gave us the Word, and lives on the inside of us. In this battle of where our life will be built on and in, we have to know and have a relationship with God.

Many of us don't have a great understanding of what it means to have a relationship with God. With all that we are taught in life about God being this great and mighty concept, or even an angry and strict old man, it's hard to imagine wanting a real relationship with him, or even thinking that it's possible to have it. But as scripture shows us, it's completely possible, and available to us all.

We first need to understand that having a relationship with His people was always on God's heart. From the very first human, to us today, God has wanted relationship with people. In fact, I would argue that that is the entire reason that He created humans and the earth in the first place.

"Then God said, "Let Us make man in Our image, according to Our likeness; let them have dominion over the fish of the sea, over the birds of the air, and over the cattle, over all the earth and over every creeping thing that creeps on the earth"" *(Genesis 1:26 NKJV).*

This is the staple verse for understanding that we are all made in God's image. But it is also the verse that proves that God created us for relationship.

A human would never have the same relationship with a fish, as they would with another human. Neither would a cat have the same relationship with a dog as they would with another cat. We are all drawn to relationship and connection with one of our own kind, and our own likeness. When God created all of the animals, He didn't give them the ability to think like humans. He gave them more strength, speed, and adaptability, but He didn't give them the ability to think clearly and intellectually. This was reserved for the humans that He made in His image. This, I believe is one of the main things that we have in common with the Lord, that even make relationship with Him possible. We can think and commune with Him in a way that the other creations cannot.

We can also look at scriptures later, in the New Testament, that explore this idea even more. Take a look at the Gospel of John.

"For God so loved the world that He gave His only begotten Son, that whoever believes in Him should not perish but have everlasting life" (John 3:16 NKJV).

"And this is eternal life, that they may know You, the only true God, and Jesus Christ whom You have sent" (John 17:3 NKJV).

The Gospel of John takes a look at the life and ministry of Jesus in a way that we don't see anywhere else. It reflects much on the character and nature of Jesus, versus what He says and does. That is shown through these verses that depict the relational aspect of God.

In John 3:16, we see that Jesus came to give us eternal life (some translations say everlasting life). The next verse tells us that eternal life is knowing God and knowing Jesus. This means that the entire reason that Jesus came down to us, was to have a relationship with us and give us an opportunity to know Him on a deep, personal level.

This is radical and goes against much of what Christianity has taught us. We often view our lives as Christians through the lens of a righteous Jew. We have to obey the law, and its commandments, or God won't want to have anything to do with us. If we sin, we will have to pay the consequences. If we don't sin, it won't be long before we do and are in trouble again. But Jesus teaches us something different than the typical pharisee would've.

Jesus wanted relationship with us, so He came down and sacrificed himself, knowing that we couldn't have made a good enough sacrifice on our own. True eternal salvation required the only perfect sacrifice, Him. In doing so, He made it possible for us to have relationship with Him, without the threat of sin constantly coming in the way of it. Knowing this, it's clear that having a relationship with God is available to us all, and something that we can walk in, every single day.

From here, we must know two different, but connecting parts of walking in relationship with Him. The first is Christian disciplines. These include Bible reading, going to Church, being in Church community, prayer, and more. There are many Christian disciplines that we can implement into our lives, but the most important thing about them is simply communing with Him.

One example of Christian discipline is mediating on the Word, which we have previously discussed. It is a way for us to commune with Him through His Word and receive revelation through the Spirit. It is a great way to not only commune with God, but also renew your mind and learn more about the Bible.

Another important Christian discipline is praying. It is our way of talking to God and pouring out our heart to Him. When we pray, we invite God into our lives and we allow what is inside of our hearts to be poured out to Him. Prayer also encourages us to bring our faith to others, and bring God into every single area of our lives.

Church and community is another great form of Christian discipline. God didn't make us to be alone. He made us to be around others and to be in relationship with others, as well as Himself. That is why the Church is so crucial for a Christian. It allow us to be around other believers that share a love for Christ, and it brings the body of Christ together, fostering unity and love. I once heard it said that because we are all made in the image of God. So, getting to know more Christians and building relationships with them is kind of like getting to see a greater picture of who God is.

While there are many Christian disciplines out there, it's crucial to look at the motive of your heart. When you practice these disciplines, are you trying to earn something? Are you after blessings and protection? Do you just want to make sure you are in right standing with God? Or, are you after a relationship with God?

David, one of the most famous names of the entire Bible, was called "a man after God's own heart". He lived a life that was faithful to God, aside from a few mistakes, and he always pursued the Lord and the Lord's heart. Most Old Testament heroes were in fear of the Lord and knew of His great and mighty power, and David was not any different. But David was one of few that pursued the Lord himself, and knew that the heart of God was not to hurt His people, but to commune with them, and deliver them. Thus, he worshiped God like no other.

Like David, are you after the heart of God? David still feared

God, and didn't overlook His greatness. But he kept his eyes on the heart of God, pursuing relationship with Him. His reverence for God even drove David to cling to Him more.

This brings us to the next key part of having relationship with God. In addition to practicing Christian disciplines, we must learn also to abide in Christ.

The simplest way to define "abiding" is to remain in Him. This can mean a bunch of different things. It can mean that you practice the disciplines so much that you stay in his presence, and His Words are on your mind, all the time. It can also mean that Christ is such a major part of your life that your life itself is dictated by Him and changes according to Him. Maybe it means that your entire life revolves around him. Your friends, your habits, your hobbies and how you act and live are all based on Jesus.

Whatever definition that you have for abiding and staying in Christ, it all means the same thing. It means that Christ is what your life depends on. Your strength and foundation comes from Him and He restores, replenishes, and refreshes you. To abide in Christ, means that He is the focal point. If we are the planets, He is the sun, and we revolve around Him. He is our source, our beginning and our end.

There are many ways to describe abiding in Christ. But the process of actually doing so is not as easy to describe and explain. That is because abiding in Christ cannot be done by just practicing one thing. It's not done by just praying or just reading your Bible, nor can it be done by just thinking about God. Because abiding and remaining in Christ is the process of putting God at the very center of your life, it includes everything that we've talked about here, and even more. It involves praying and talking to God, reading your Bible and meditating on it, getting filled with the Spirit, learning more about your spiritual identity, and more. Whatever it takes to place the Lord at the very center of your life, and remain in Him is what it means to abide in Christ.

Abiding in Christ takes discipline and dedication to the Lord. It means that He has to be such an integral part of your thought and spiritual life that you've been affected and changed by the relationship. Your strength and foundation comes from the Lord, and the sometimes "distant" feeling God, feels more like a close friend.

David abided in Christ, preemptively of course. His life was based upon the Lord. We see him go back to the Lord time and time again, often with cries of pain, and shouts of praise. Even within the same Psalm at times. He genuinely pursued the heart of God, just as we must fervently pursue relationship with Christ.

To abide in Christ, is the conclusion of what it means to be rooted in Him. In fact, some could argue that those that are truly abiding in Christ, are rooted in Him, because it is from the place of remaining in Christ that you start to be changed and portray the fruit of who one is rooted in Him.

Understanding Spirit, Soul, and Body, and knowing that we are fighting a much bigger, yet unseen battle is part of being in Christ. Knowing the power of our minds and the thoughts that can change our entire life is key to remaining in Christ. Practicing the Christian disciplines, knowing the truth and mediating on the truth is certainly part of abiding in Christ, and possibly the most important aspect of abiding is having a genuine relationship with God. These are all the necessary steps towards being rooted in Christ, as well as remaining in Him.

It is from this place of remaining in Christ, and rooting ourselves deeper into the character and nature of God, that we can find strength and peace. It is from this place, where we can build a life, on a solid foundation where the storms of life and the attacks of any enemy cannot harm us.

""Therefore whoever hears these sayings of Mine, and does them, I will liken him to a wise man who built his house on the rock: and the rain descended, the floods came, and the winds blew and beat on that house; and it did not fall, for it was founded on the rock" (Matthew 7:24-25 NKJV).

To live a life that displays the fruit of Christ, and provides strength, peace, and Among, we must live our lives in constant relationship with Christ. He must be more than a religion to us. He must be more than a friend, even more than a father. He must be our lord, our life, and our rock. He must be that whom we plant ourselves in, and whom we are built up in.

There are many blessings that come from rooting yourself in Christ, and developing a strong relationship with Him. Blessings that you will not find in a church, in a car, or in any fleeting, carnal thing. These blessings go deeper than what we can see, and they are not just for us, but for the entire world.

Bearing New Fruit

N ow that we are aware of how we are to be rooted in Christ, we must recognize the importance of it in our lives, and how it affects both our lives with Christ, and our lives with others.

Being rooted in Christ is not just a Christian discipline in itself, but it is the practice of the Christian life. Those that say they follow Christ must learn to be rooted in Him, if they are to bear the name of Christ in their lives. It isn't an optional thing like devotionals or even community groups. It's a necessity. The path towards rooting ourselves in Christ is something that every Christian must walk. Those that do not, will live their lives still striving for perfection and for acceptance, working to do good and prove themselves, while those that are rooted in Him daily will simply do good and live free from the overflow of their life with God.

Rooting yourself in Christ is the essential aspect of Christianity that we often see missing in today's Church. It does many things for the Christian and it changes us from the inside out. Without it, we won't be prepared for what God has for us, and we won't ever become the Christ-like people that the world desperately needs.

Among the many powerful things that rooting ourselves in

Christ does for us, there are three key processes that we must notice. The first is the breaking of the fallow ground. In order for us to be rooted in Christ in the first place, the fallow or uncultivated ground must be broken up, in order for the seeds of righteousness to be planted.

"Sow for yourselves righteousness; reap in mercy, break up your fallow ground, for it is time to seek the Lord, till He comes and rains righteousness on you" (Hosea 10:12 NKJV).

""Break up your fallow ground, and do not sow among thorns"" (Jeremiah 4:3 NKJV).

When we are away from God, or new to the faith, there is fallow or uncultivated ground in our heart that has been riddled with thorns, hardened and been left unused for righteousness. By seeking the Lord and allowing Him to soften your heart, clearing the thorns and bristles, and giving you a fresh, clean heart, you allow for seeds of righteousness to be sown in your heart, and the Word of God to come in and change you.

The breaking of the fallow and hardened ground allows for the things of God, such as the Word to dwell deep in your heart and sow a harvest of righteousness.

Once your heart has been greater prepared for everything that God wants to plant in your heart and in your life, you begin to bear fruit. As we've discussed, the fruit of the Spirit, as by having been rooted in Christ, you will be walking in the Spirit, is love, joy, peace, patience, kindness, goodness, faithfulness, and self control (Galatians 5:22-23). This means that by rooting yourself in Christ, you can now begin to bear fruit for Christ.

"I am the vine, you are the branches. He who abides in Me, and I in him, bears much fruit; for without Me you can do nothing. If anyone does not abide in Me, he is cast out as a branch and is withered; and they gather them and throw them into the fire, and they are burned. If you abide in Me, and My words abide in you, you will ask what you desire, and it shall be done for you. By this My Father is glorified, that you bear much fruit; so you will be My disciples" *(John 15:5-8 NKJV).*

When we root ourselves in Christ and abide in Him, we can begin to bear fruit for Him and His kingdom. What was sown in us as seed through Christ, is now ready to blossom into fruit that can be a blessing for ourselves, others, and Christ. Like an apple tree follows the apple seed planted, we begin to bear fruit following the seeds planted by walking with Christ. However, the fruit that we produce isn't just any fruit, but it is like the fruit that Christ portrayed as shown in 1 John.

"By this we know that we are in Him. He who says he abides in Him ought himself also to walk just as He walked" *(1 John 2:5-6 NKJV).*

This verse opens us up to many questions and theories, but it's meaning seems to be very clear. This verse tells us that by simply staying in Christ, walking in relationship with Him, and rooting ourselves in Him, we can walk and live as He did. If that doesn't sound almost too-good-to-be-true, then let me remind you how Jesus lived.

Throughout His time on Earth, Jesus lived a perfect sin-less life. He performed miracles, rose the dead, healed the sick, cast out demons and more. Jesus lived His life for others and for the

Father. He always had plenty, but was able to stand for forty days with no food, so certainly He knew how to have little, and how to have much. Now, through His spirit, and by rooting ourselves in Him, we are able to live and walk just as He did. The ability to live sin-less and do miraculous things has been passed to us and is simply a byproduct of rooting ourselves in Him. That is surely too-good-to-be-true news.

But it's true! Jesus makes all these things and more available to us, and uses us to help bring upon his great and perfect will. But it is only by staying in Him, and walking daily with Him, that these things will ever be able to come about, and He can only use us as much as we are able to be used. If we aren't in daily communion with God, and practicing the Christian disciplines, how are we going to hear His voice, and know who to pray for or how to pray. If his word isn't on the inside of our hearts and renewing our mind, how is He going to remind us of a scripture to pray for or to strength our faith for the good works? In order for the good fruit to be born in our lives, we must start by rooting ourselves in Him.

Now, as we live in Christ and continually put ourselves in Him, we will be changed and will began to display the good fruit. We don't need to try super hard to display the fruit that Christ produced, we just need to work to keep ourselves in Him. We can't do good things out of the very nature of our own hearts, and we certainly can't live the life that Jesus has called us to live on our own. We must stay in Christ, rooted and built up in Him, and allow Him to display the good fruit that He longs to share with the world.

"But we all, with unveiled face, beholding as in a mirror the glory of the Lord, are being transformed into the same

image from glory to glory, just as by the Spirit of the Lord"(2 Corinthians 3:18 NKJV).

The Christian life includes more than a belief system and a weekly church service. It includes living and being transformed into God's same image, the image of Jesus, little by little. By "beholding" and looking upon the nature and character of God through communion and scripture reading, we are slowly being transformed into God's image, displaying the same fruit that Jesus displayed and walking just as He walked. Of course, this happens little by little, day by day, but we are certainly being miraculously transformed by the living God.

Which leads us to the final major process that happens as we are rooted in Christ, and keeping ourselves in Him. That is a pruning process.

Pruning is the practice of cutting away unwanted parts, such as branches, roots, or stems, from plants and trees. It is done for a variety of reasons, from the look and aesthetic, to the actual growth and structure of the overall plant. The main reason, however, is to increase the fruitfulness of the plant, as the pruning process cuts out the dead or diseased parts. Certainly, you can see how this relates to the Christian "rooted in Christ" life.

""I am the true vine, and My Father is the vine dresser. Every branch in Me that does not bear fruit He takes away; and every branch that bears fruit He prunes, that it may bear more fruit"" *(John 15:1-2 NKJV).*

We don't see many verses about being pruned throughout scripture, but we do have this powerful parable. Here, Jesus relates to Himself as the one true vine. This makes us the branches on the vine that are connected and dependent upon the vine itself for life and provision. This also makes God the Father the vine dresser, who takes care of the vines and branches. God does all of the pruning and cutting, taking away what is unneeded of the branches, and allowing the branches to produce a greater, more fruitful harvest. This parable not only reflects how we are to be in Christ, by showing that Jesus is the only true vine and that to be alive spiritually, we must be a part of Him, but it is also shows us the pruning process.

There are things in our life, branches, that God must cut away. These things are either not fruitful, dead, or unusable. By cutting these bad parts away, we are able to be more fruitful for Christ, and display more of Him in our lives.

Think about something that God took away in your life. Before I was walking with Christ and living in Him, I would get mad. It wasn't something that was very expressive, but I would foster aggression and pent up bitterness. As I begin to allow God into my life, those feelings and habits started to go away, and that was something that God pruned from my life. As I've dove deeper into my relationship with Christ, depression, anxiety, and self-reliance have been taken away as well. I've also noticed that my effectiveness for the kingdom has since increased and I've displayed more fruit. But if the Lord never took away all that had previously held me back, I wouldn't be able to show the fruit that I have, or live like I have. I desperately needed the Lord to prune me, and to remove what was previously holding me back from bearing fruit.

What is holding you back from bearing fruit? What does the Lord need to prune and cut away? Perhaps it is the deeds of the flesh, as Galatians 5 puts it. Do you struggle with jealousy, sexual immorality, idolatry, or fits of anger? We all struggle with something, and all have dead or unwanted things in our lives that need the Lord's attention. By rooting ourselves in Him, walking in relationship with Him, and practicing the Christian disciplines, we can not only know those things that need to be removed, but we can allow the Lord to remove them for us.

In doing this, we can bear more fruit for Christ, the long list of which includes reflecting Christ in our communities, doing miraculous acts, and evangelizing for the sake of the gospel. So, here is where we find the very purpose of the Christian life. Among the many directions and instructions we are given, we are told of two things with the highest importance. To love God, and to love others, as ourselves. The "rooted in Christ" life, empowers you to do both, as only those that are truly rooted in Christ, are built up in love, able to understand the fullness of love, and walk out in it.

"-that Christ may dwell in your hearts through faith; that you, being rooted and grounded in love, may be able to comprehend with all the saints what is the width and length and depth and height— to know the love of Christ which passes knowledge; that you may be filled with all the fullness of God" (Ephesians 3:17-19 NKJV).

"As you therefore have received Christ Jesus the Lord, so walk in Him, rooted and built up in Him and established in the faith, as you have been taught, abounding in it with thanksgiving" (Colossians 2:6-7 NKJV).

I say then, that the Christian life can be summed up in one practice. That is, rooting yourself in Christ, and staying in Him daily.